Walt Disney Pictures Presents

Aladdin

Arranged by Shannon M. Grama

ISBN 0-7935-1874-1

Hal Leonard Publishing Corporation
7777 West Bluemound Road P.O. Box 13819 Milwaukee, WI 53213

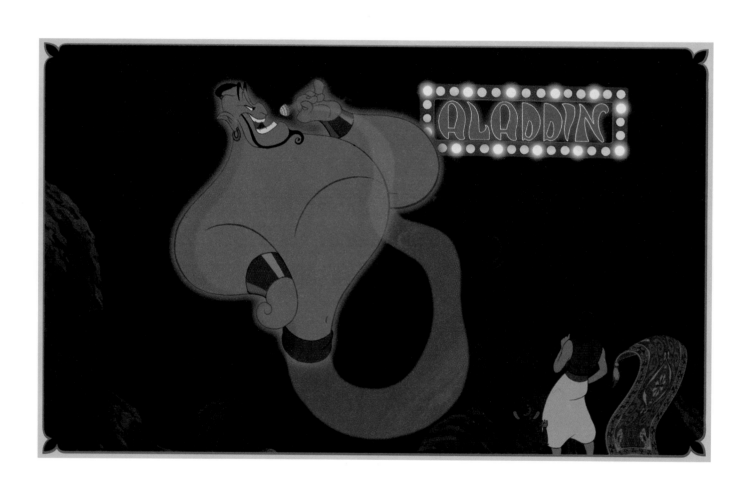

Aladdin

ARABIAN NIGHTS

Words by HOWARD ASHMAN
Music by ALAN MENKEN

Moderately bright

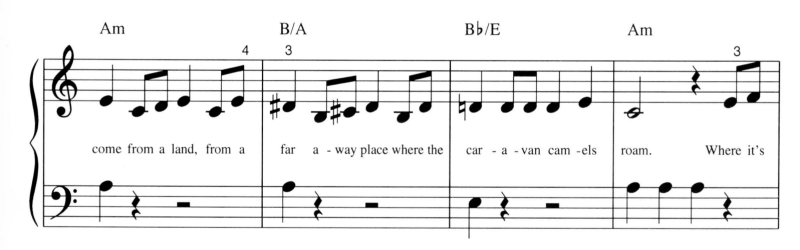

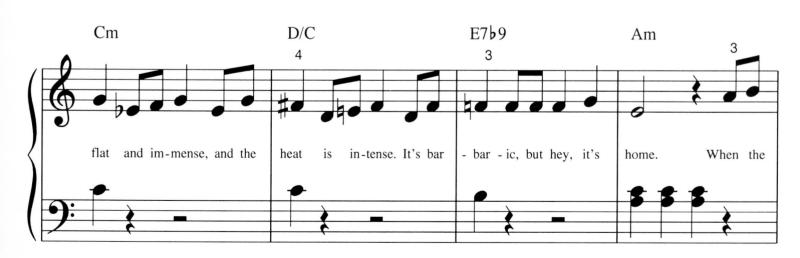

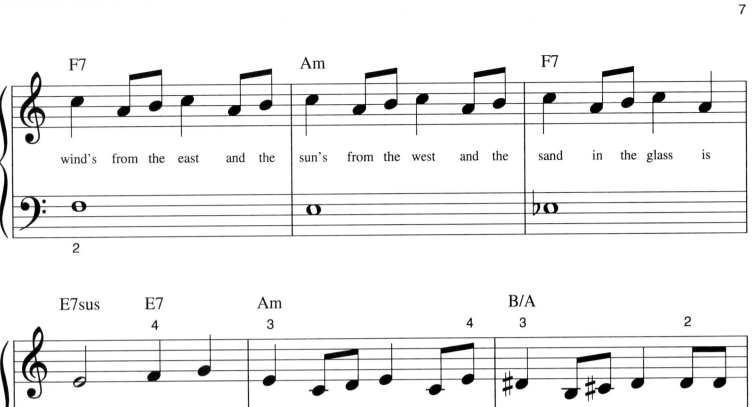

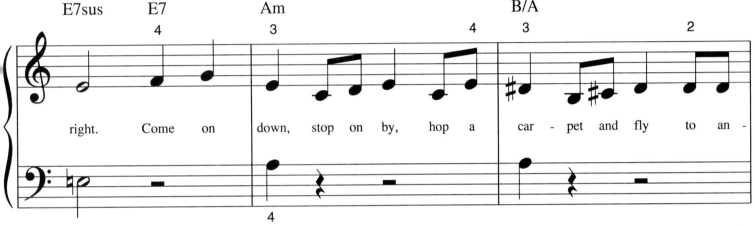

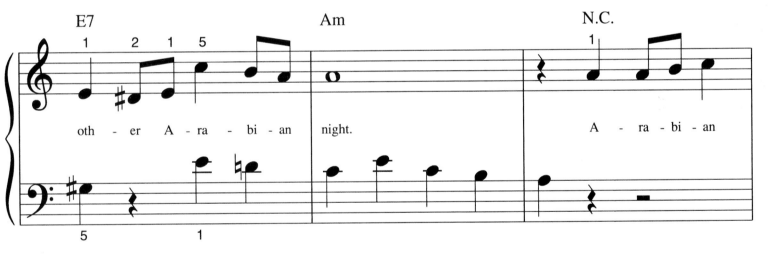

ONE JUMP AHEAD

Music by ALAN MENKEN
Words by TIM RICE

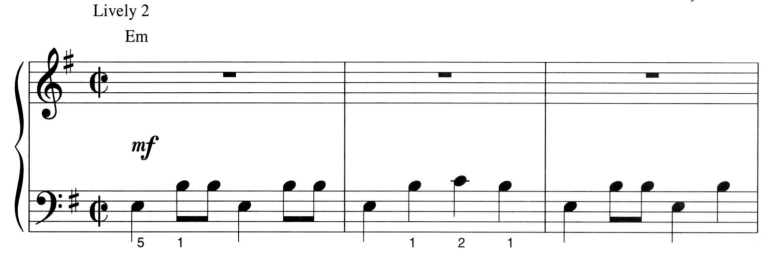

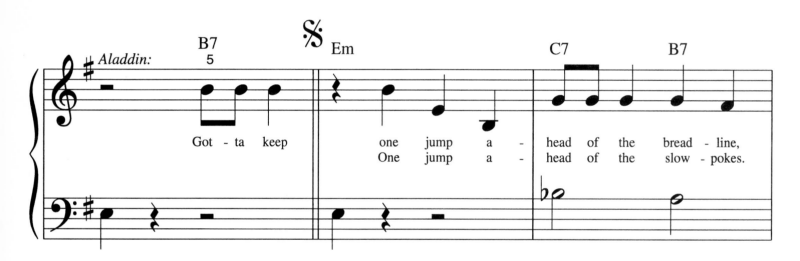

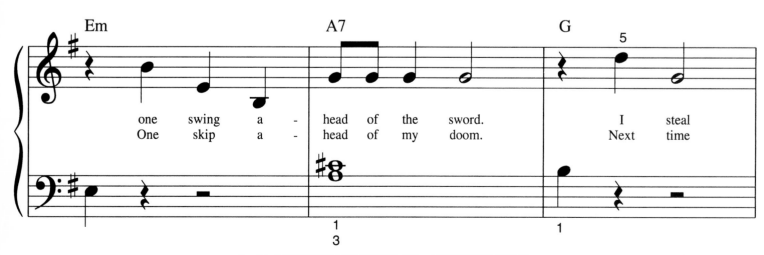

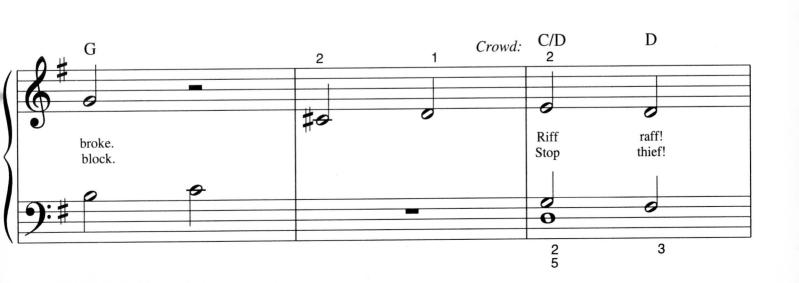

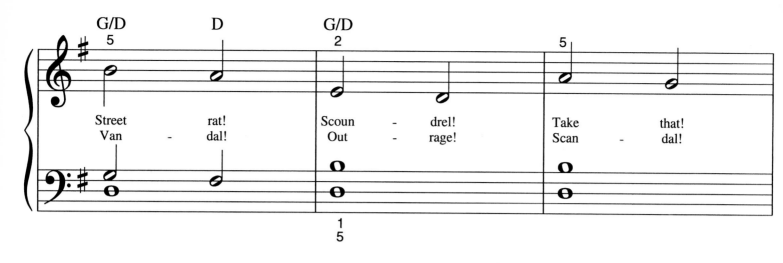

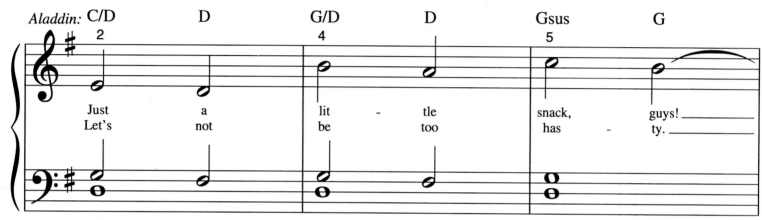

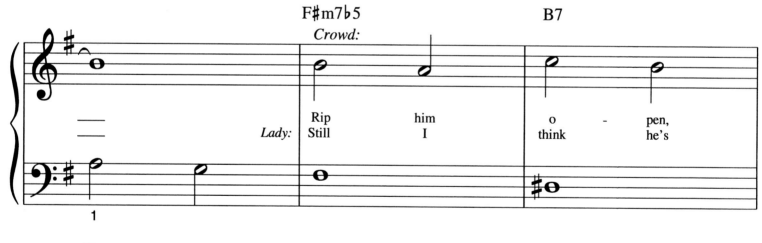

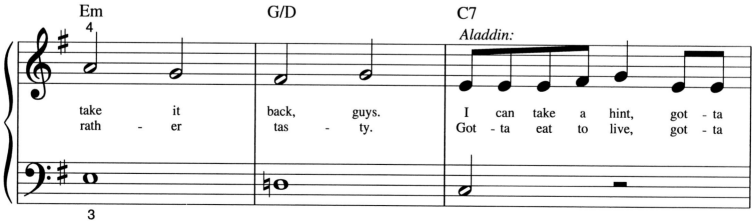

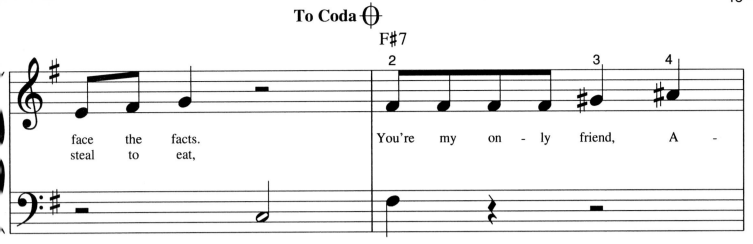

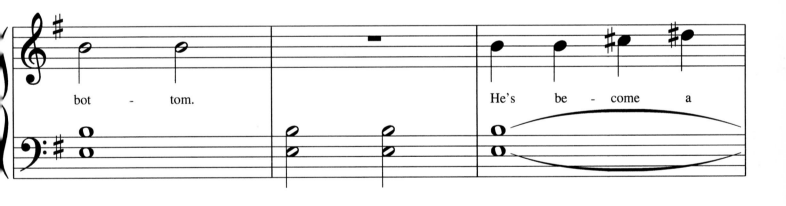

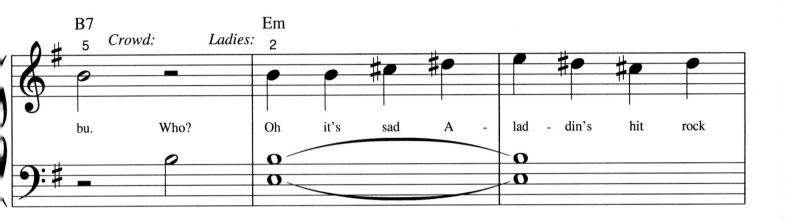

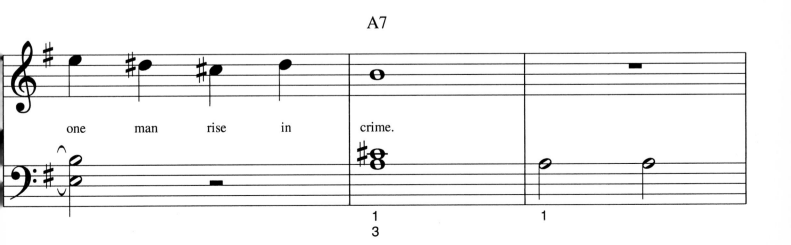

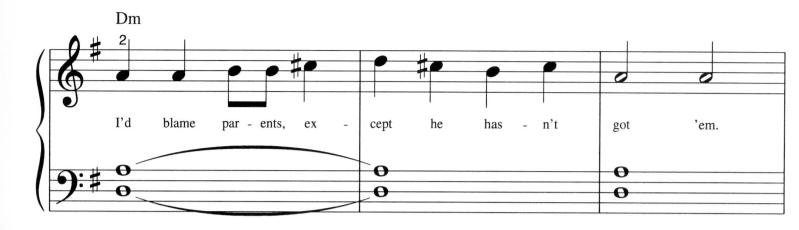

Dm

I'd blame par - ents, ex - cept he has - n't got 'em.

F#7

Aladdin:

Got - ta eat to live, got - ta steal to eat, tell you all a -

B7

D.S. al Coda

bout it when I got the time.

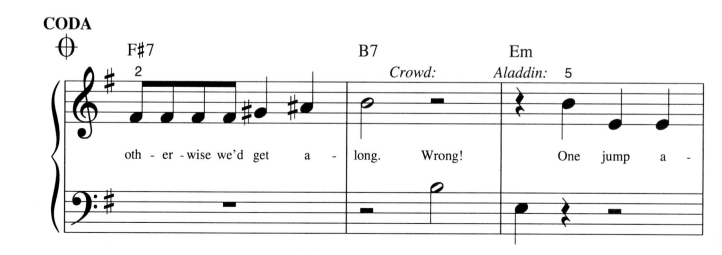

CODA

F#7

B7

Em

Crowd:

Aladdin:

oth - er - wise we'd get a - long. Wrong! One jump a -

ONE JUMP AHEAD
(Reprise)

Music by ALAN MENKEN
Words by TIME RICE

Slowly and freely

Riff raff, street rat, I don't buy that. If

on - ly they'd look clos - er, would they see a

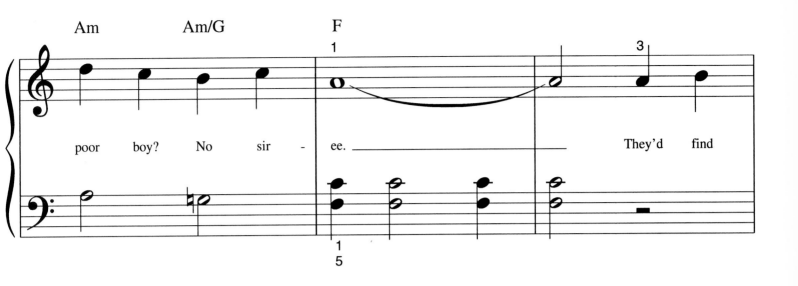

poor boy? No sir - ee. _____ They'd find

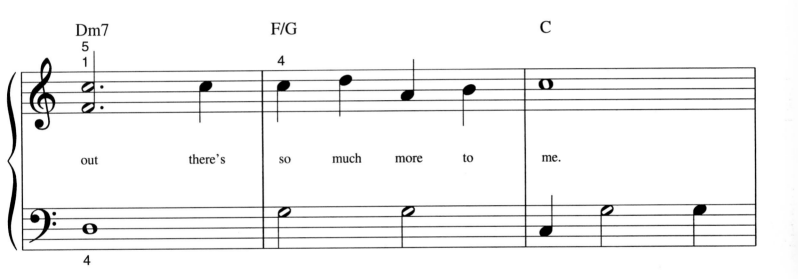

out there's so much more to me.

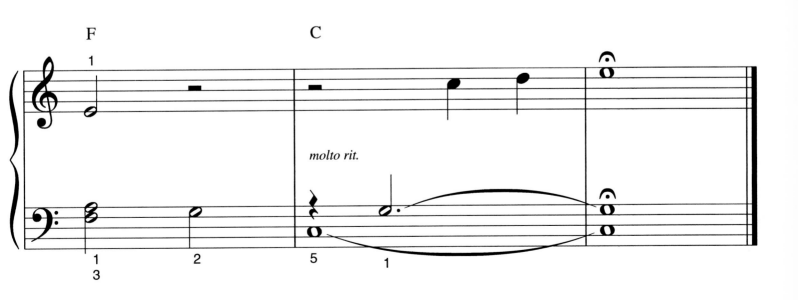

molto rit.

FRIEND LIKE ME

Words by HOWARD ASHMAN
Music by ALAN MENKEN

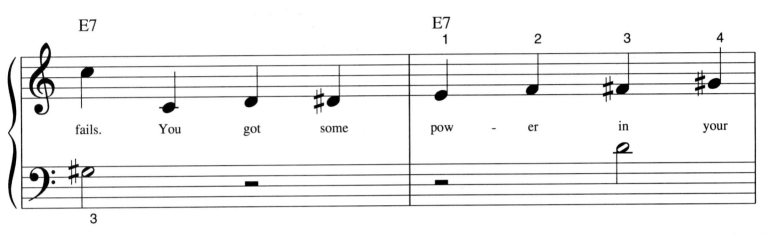

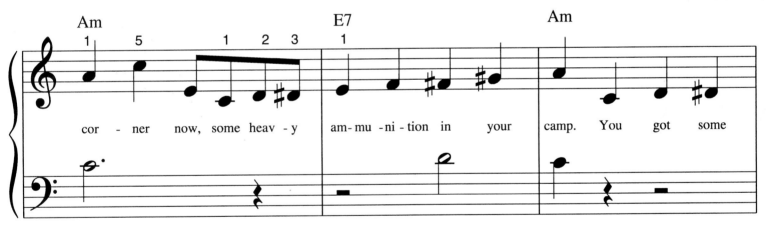

22

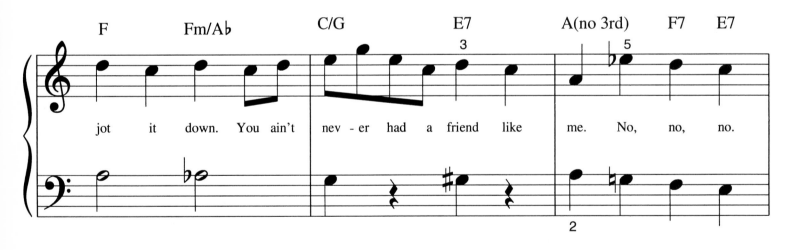

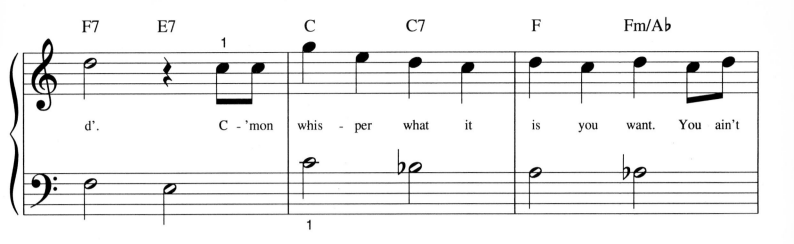

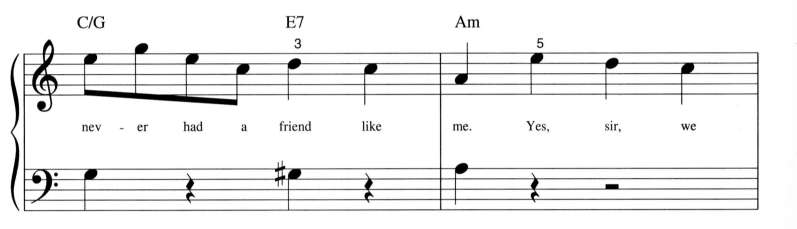

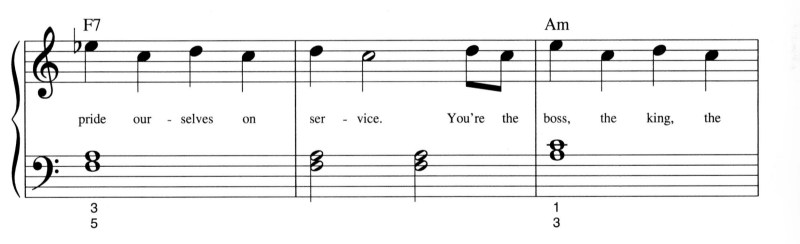

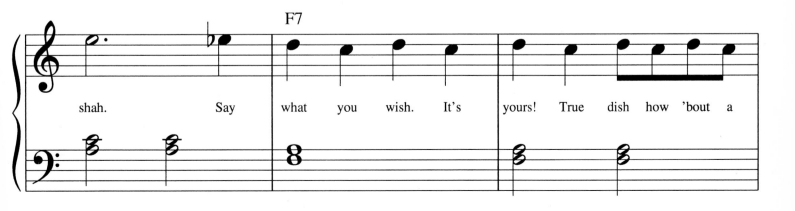

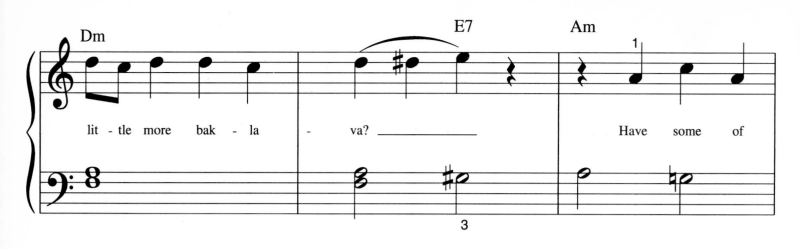

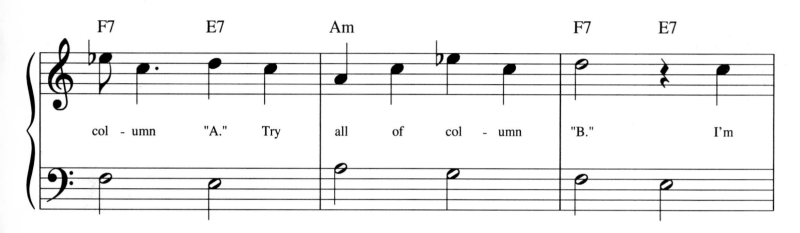

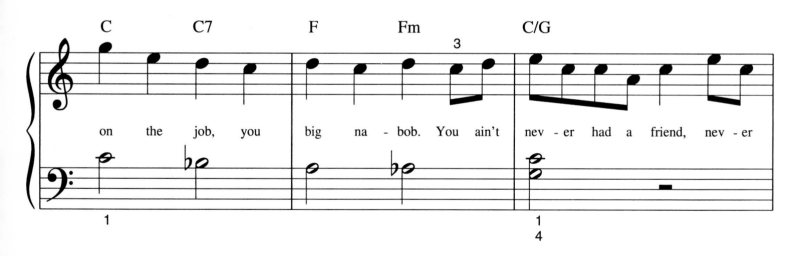

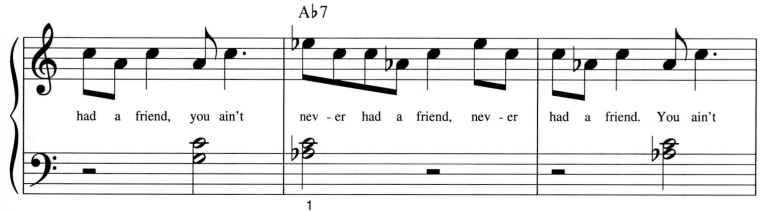

PRINCE ALI

Words by HOWARD ASHMAN
Music by ALAN MENKEN

In two, not fast

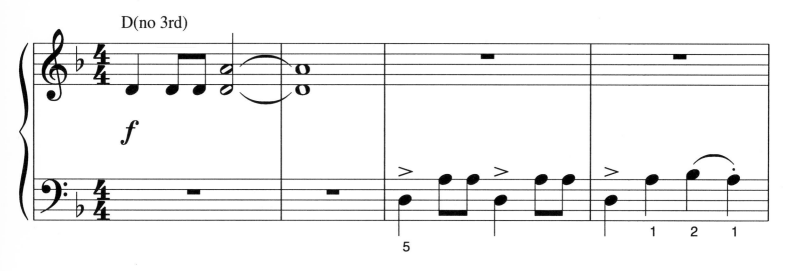

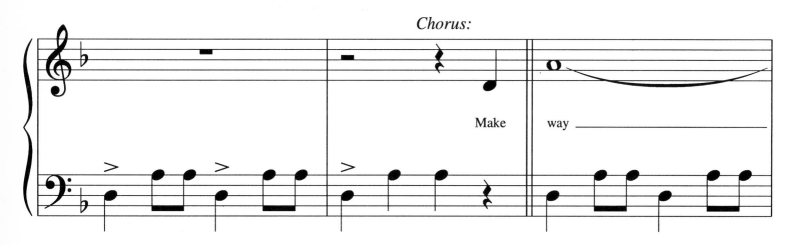

Chorus:

Make way _____

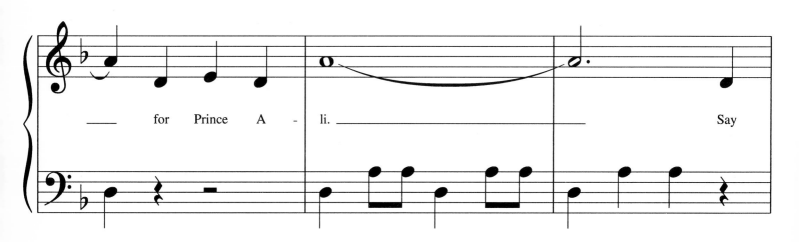

_____ for Prince A - li. _____ Say

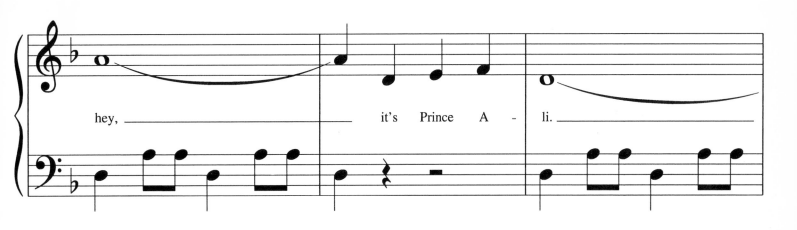

hey, _____ it's Prince A - li. _____

Genie: Dm

Hey! Clear the way in the old Ba - zaar. Hey

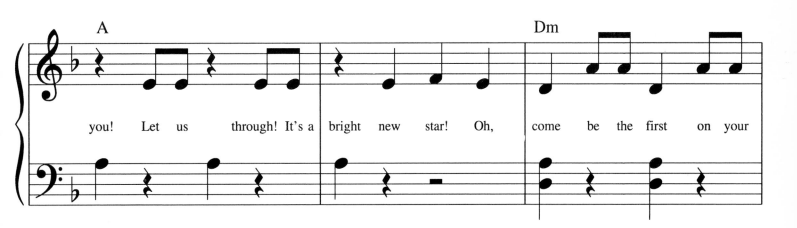

A

Dm

you! Let us through! It's a bright new star! Oh, come be the first on your

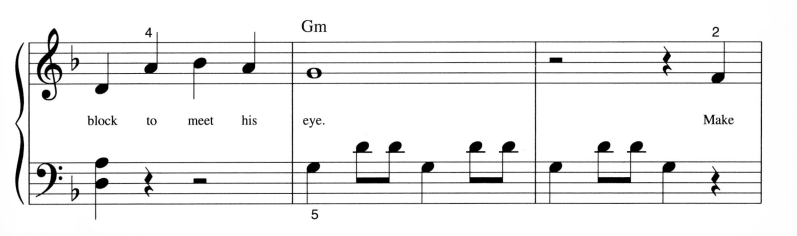

Gm

block to meet his eye. Make

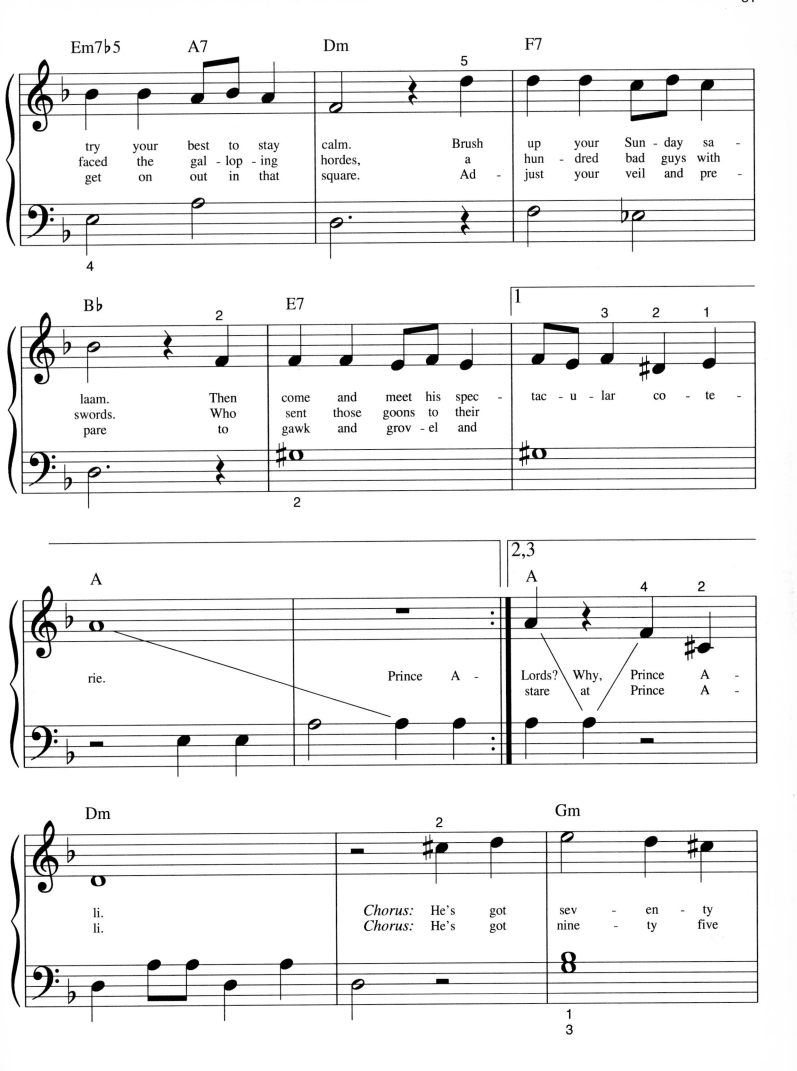

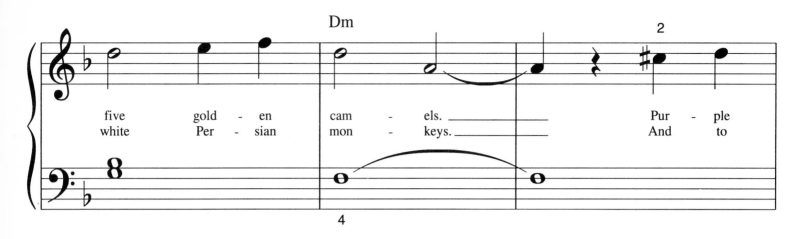

five gold - en cam - els. _____ Pur - ple
white Per - sian mon - keys. _____ And to

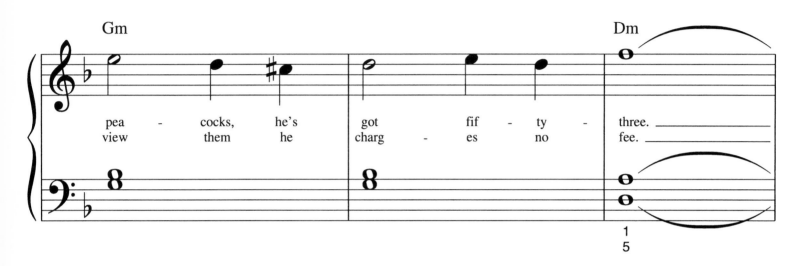

pea - cocks, he's got fif - ty - three. _____
view them he charg - es no fee. _____

Genie:

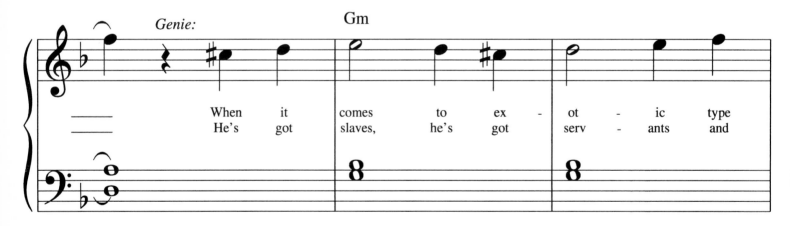

_____ When it comes to ex - ot - ic type
He's got slaves, he's got serv - ants and

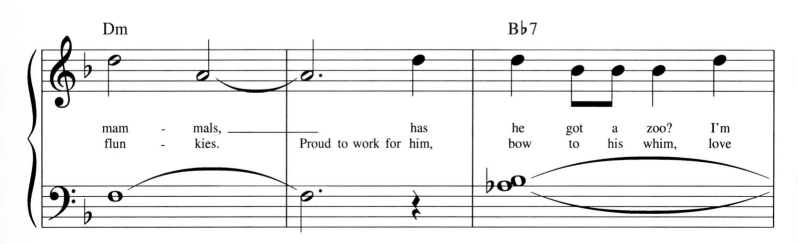

mam - mals, _____ has he got a zoo? I'm
flun - kies. Proud to work for him, bow to his whim, love

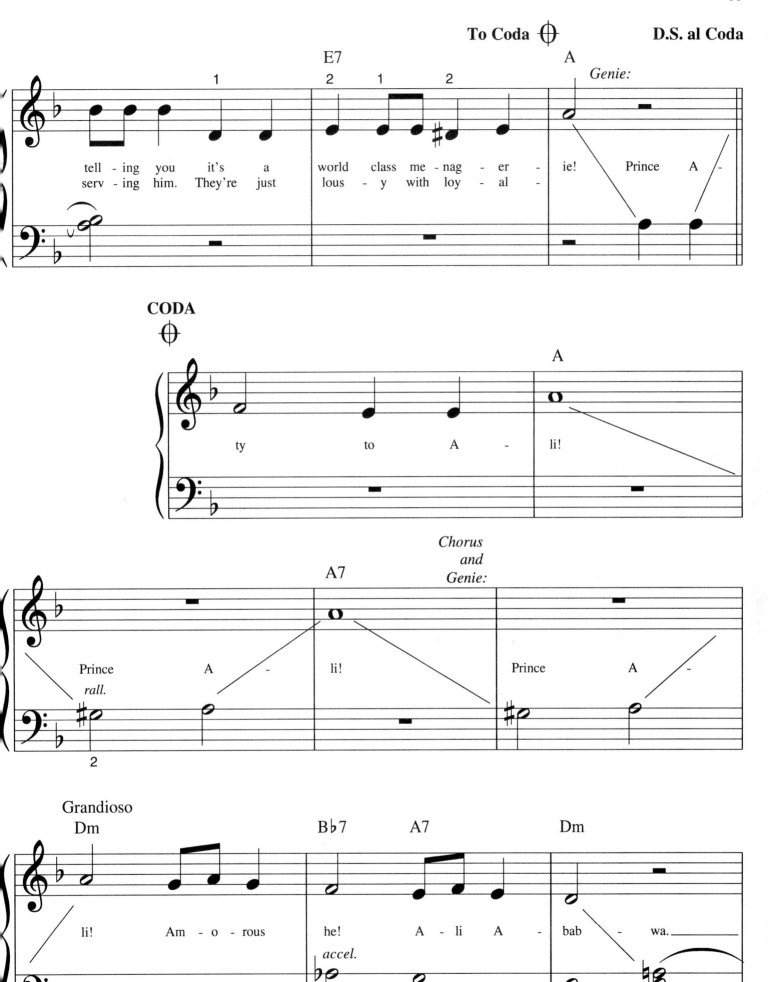

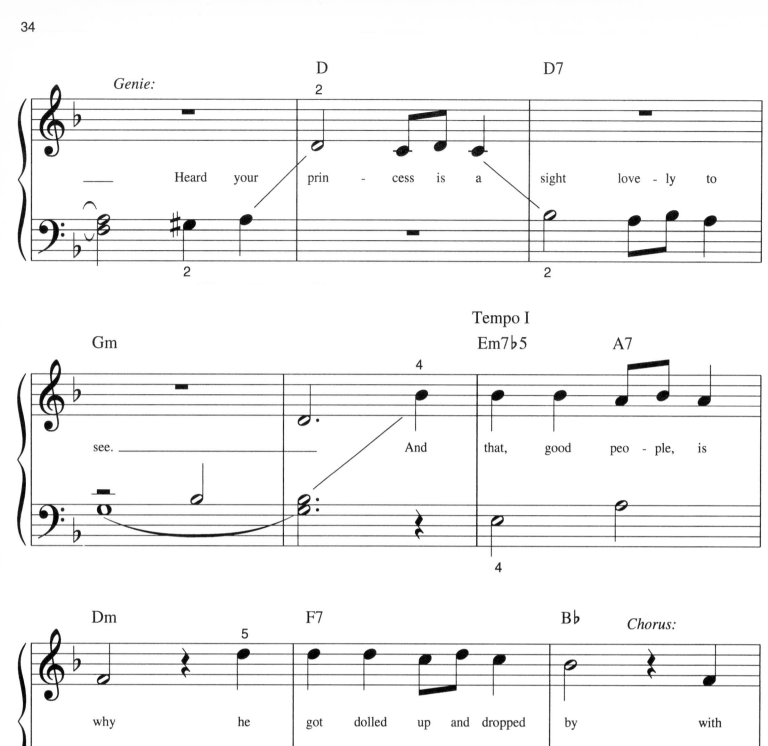

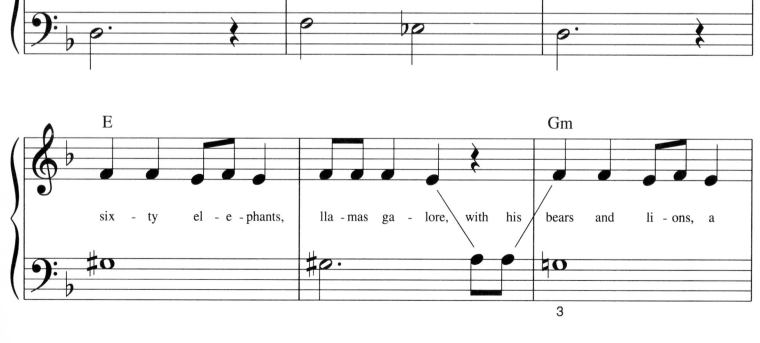

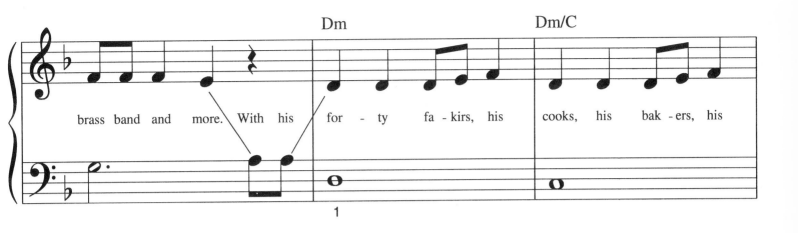

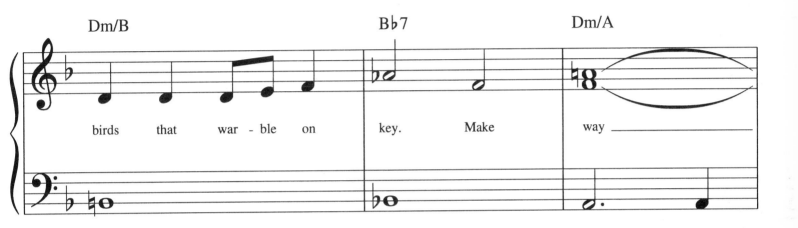

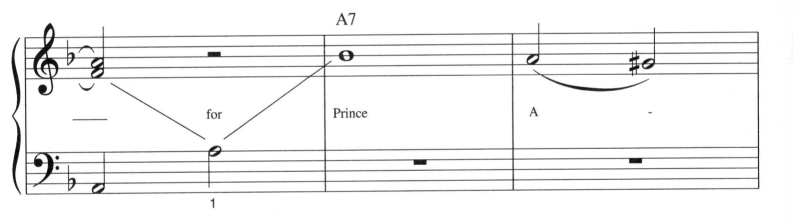

A WHOLE NEW WORLD

Music by ALAN MENKEN
Words by TIM RICE

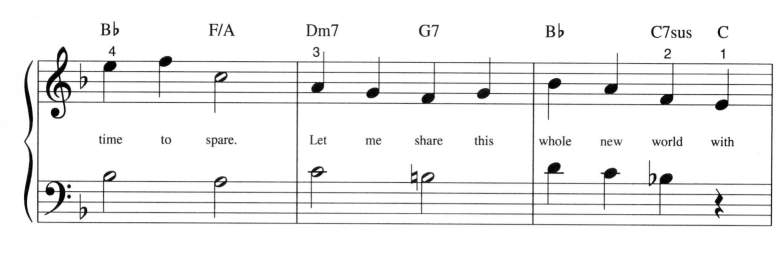

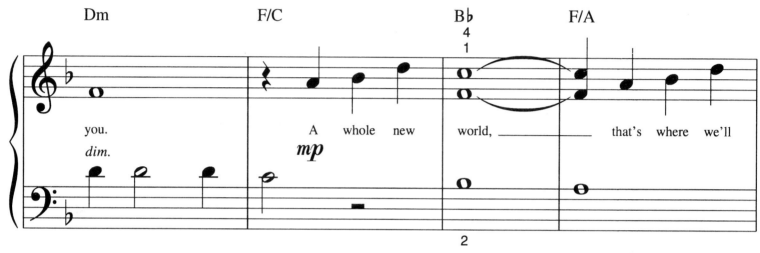

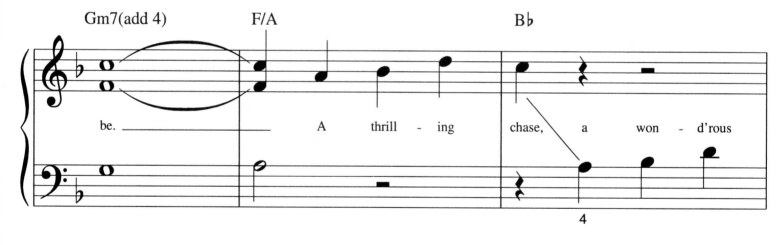

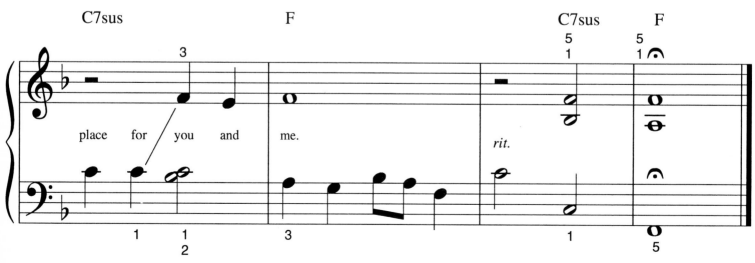

PRINCE ALI
(Reprise)

Music by ALAN MENKEN
Words by TIM RICE

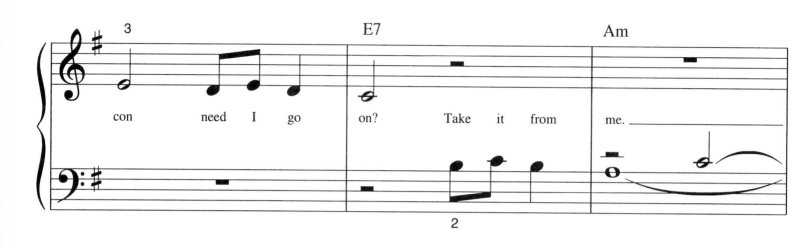

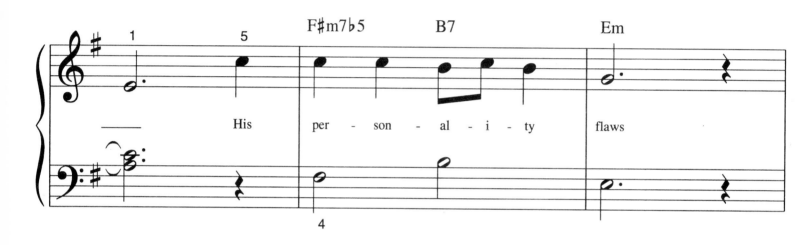

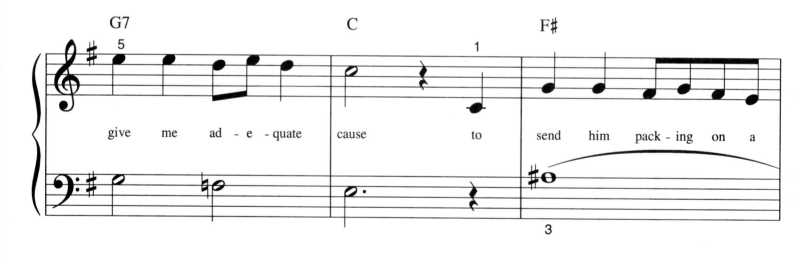

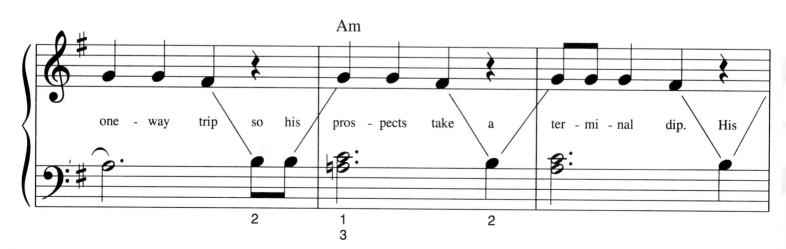

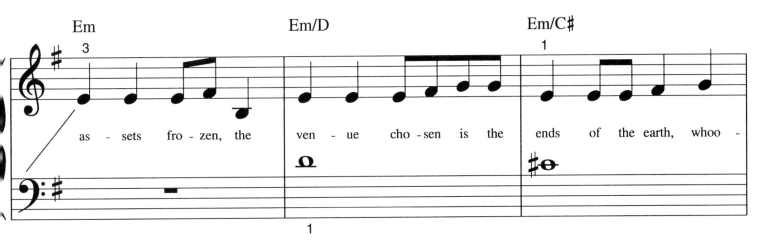

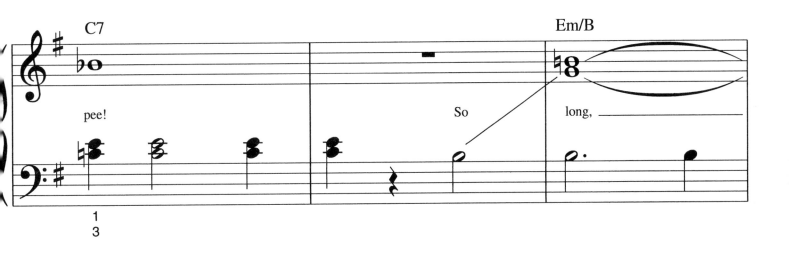

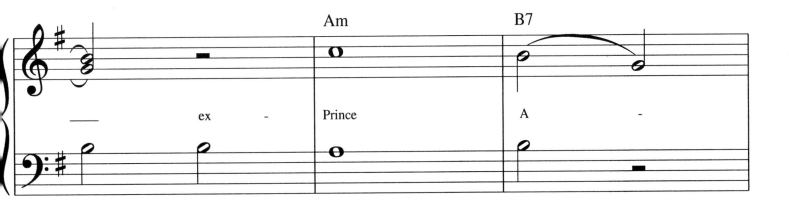

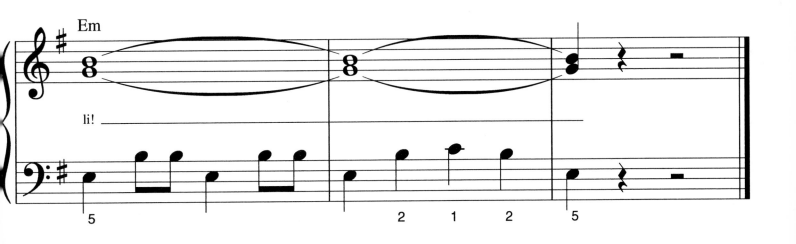